SCROLL SAW RELIEF

By Marilyn Carmin

FOX BOOKS
Fox Chapel Publishing Co Inc.

1970 Broad Street
East Petersburg, PA 17520

Publisher: Alan Giagnocavo
Project Editor: Ayleen Stellhorn
Desktop Specialist: Linda L. Eberly, Eberly Designs Inc.
Interior Photography: Robert Polett
Cover Photography: Robert Polett

ISBN # 1-56523-107-4

To order your copy of this book,
please send check or money order
for $14.95 plus $2.50 shipping to:
Fox Books
1970 Broad Street
East Petersburg, PA 17520

Manufactured in the United States

DEDICATION

To my family and friends: You encourage me to reach for the sky and the stars beyond.
To my brother, Mark: I could not have done this without you!
To my husband, Garth: Your love, encouragement and belief in me have been
    my "solid rock" to hold onto.
Thank you all!

Table of Contents

ABOUT THE AUTHOR

Marilyn Carmin has been using the scroll saw for over sixteen years and designing patterns for almost as long. Her favorite technique is relief, and she enjoys combining it with fret. Marilyn is the designer for Heartland Creations, a scroll saw pattern company specializing in wildlife. She also does some freelance designing for periodicals. For a Heartland Creations catalog, call 1-360-686-3133.

Relief Cutting

Frames, mirrors, furniture and many other projects can be beautifully enhanced by using relief cutting. The natural effect of relief cutting gives projects a "carved" appearance. This is accomplished by portions of the design being raised or recessed with angled cuts.

Most scroll saw tables are designed to adjust for angle cutting. The degree of a table's angle, combined with the direction of the cut, give the relief effect.

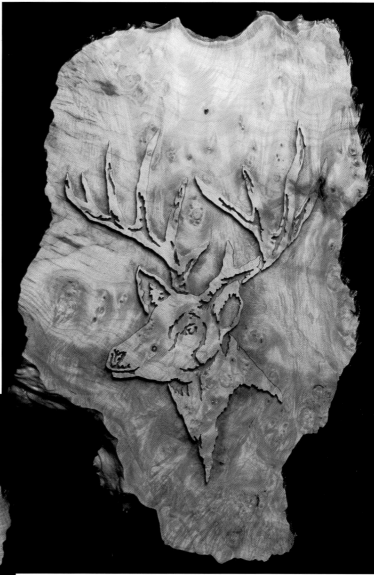

Natural burl complements wildlife. This deer is cut from a maple burl. All pieces within pieces are cut first.

Tea Time is cut using an all relief technique. Start with the smallest pieces first, then move to the larger pieces.

This piece of wood jewelry is titled *Springtime.* Long narrow pieces of relief need to be handled with care. You can reduce the chance of breakage by holding the pieces in place with masking tape until all the cuts are made.

CHAPTER PURPOSE

To give an understanding of relief cutting, how it is cut, and the knowledge needed to create patterns.

TECHNIQUE

The brand of scroll saw used can create some limitations. Although not absolutely necessary, it is preferable to have a table that angles both right and left and has gauge settings of one-degree increments. The project size is limited to the throat depth of the saw. For example, with an 18" throat depth, the wood can be no larger than 18" at its widest point.

The type of blade the saw requires can also create limitations. When pin-ended blades are used, the relief work is limited to patterns with no inside cuts. Drilled holes for pin-end blades must be large enough for the pins, which make the holes conspicuous. Projects with relief cuts starting from the edge of the wood are the best projects to tackle with pin-end blades.

In relief cutting, the angles used are small: two to four degrees. The extent of the degree determines the depth of the relief. The lower the degree, the more the relief.

Another determining factor for relief cuts is the width of the wood. The same angle in 3/4-inch wood may not allow enough wedge in a thinner wood and can create too much in a thicker wood. The width of the blade will also change the equation. A thick blade will allow more movement than a thin blade, therefore allowing a deeper cut. Patterns included in this book have a suggested setting of three degrees and a blade size of 12.5 tpi, but it is always best to cut a sample.

Before beginning a project, make a few sample cuts in a scrap from the actual project wood. Use the suggested size blade along with the suggested degree setting. By pushing the sample into relief, you can see if adjustments need to be made.

Because angles are difficult to duplicate, complete all the relief cuts before moving the table. Reset the table to 0° and finish any cutting.

If it becomes necessary to duplicate an angle, use the following method. Take a cut piece from the project, place it on the saw table and tilt the table until the cut edge and the blade are parallel. If the saw has right and left settings, make sure the table is set in the correct direction. Check by cutting another sample.

Another consideration for relief work is the direction in which the cutting is done. Cutting clockwise or counter-clockwise determines whether the piece is

Table Angle	Raised Effect	Recessed Effect
Right	Cut Clockwise	Cut Counter-Clockwise
Left	Cut Counter-Clockwise	Cut Clockwise

Illustration 1: Direction of cut will determine raised or recessed effect.

raised or recessed. (See Illustration 1.)

To cut a project that is longer than the saw's throat depth requires patience and a saw table that angles right and left. Determine the correct degree setting with sample cuts. Set the samples aside and cut as much of the pattern as possible. Back the blade out when necessary. Reset the table in the other direction using the previously discussed method. Rethread the blade through the pilot holes and complete the cutting coming from opposite direction. Although this requires extra work, it makes larger relief projects possible.

Begin a relief project by putting the pattern on the wood. Two methods for pattern application are tracing with a pencil or adhering a pattern copy with temporary bonding spray adhesive.

Drill pilot holes for any inside cuts. This can be done with the wood flat, but for best results, pilot holes should be drilled at the cutting angle. A simple way to do this is to set the saw table at the cutting angle, place the wood on the table, and then drill the hole. By holding the drill parallel to the saw blade, the holes will be at the appropriate angle. (See Illustration 2.) Caution: Don't drill into your saw table!

Using a small drill bit keeps the pilot hole inconspicuous. Bits smaller than 1/16" are numbered. A

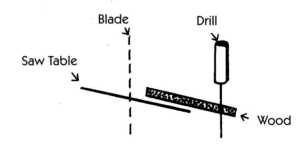

Illustration 2: The pilot hole should be drilled at the cutting angle.

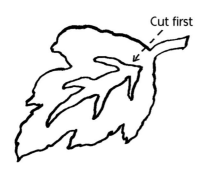

Illustration 3: Cut the inside pieces first.

number 58 or 60 is the smallest size you'll need.

Patterns in this book have directional cutting arrows near the drilling point. These need to be pointing in the cutting direction for each hole drilled. Cutting begins with the smallest piece first, working toward the largest. If the pieces are the same size, work across the project. Any pieces within pieces are cut first. (See Illustration 3.)

Long, narrow pieces need to be handled with care. Chance of breakage is reduced by holding the pieces in place until cutting is complete. As a section of the project is cut, put masking tape across it. Once all the cutting is complete, lay the project on a flat surface and remove the tape.

Finish sand the face and the back of the project. Do not sand the relief cut edges as this will affect their fit. When the sanding is complete, lift the main part of the project away leaving the cut pieces on the flat surface. The project is now ready for gluing.

Gluing holds the pieces in relief and prevents damage. Putting a thin layer of wood glue on the cut edges where those edges touch is all that is needed. A small, flat paintbrush for spreading the glue helps to keep the project free of any excess. If there is excess, lift it away with a toothpick, cotton swab or paper towel.

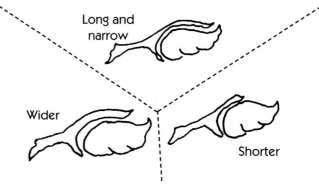

Illustration 5: Widen or shorten long and extended areas of the design.

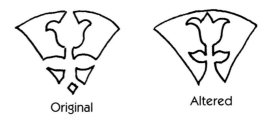

Original   Altered

Illustration 6: Connect or eliminate small areas without changing the basic design.

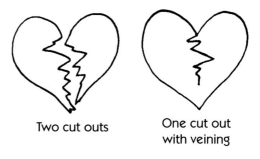

Two cut outs   One cut out with veining

Illustration 7: Use the blade width to cut definition lines eliminating a need for some cutouts.

Narrow lines   Separated lines

Illustration 4: Separate close lines, to add strength.

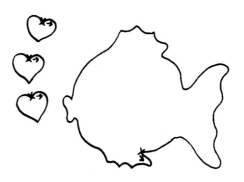

Illustration 8: Mark the pilot hole with an X and use an arrow to show cutting direction.

RELIEF

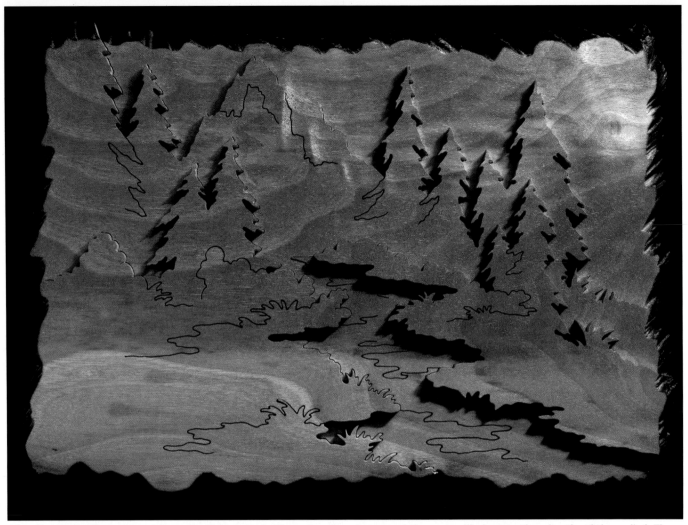

The Great Outdoors is cut from English walnut. Changing the degree of the cut will change the depth of the relief. The lower the degree, the more relief.

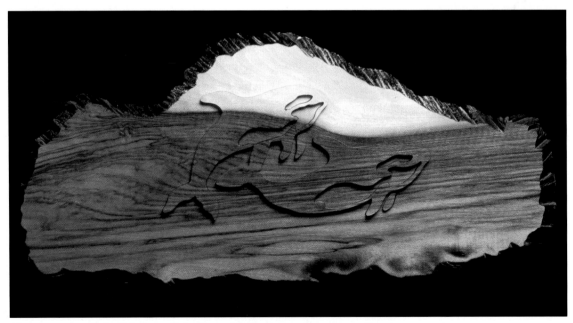

The use of grain in this "orca" design adds to the appearance of water.

The piece is inserted and pushed toward the narrow part of the cut, tightening into place. Inserting the pieces cleanly and evenly makes a large difference in the project's finished appearance.

HINTS FOR RELIEF PATTERNS

Many scroll saw patterns can be changed for relief cutting. The following are hints that will be of help when creating a relief pattern.

Close lines, long and extended cuts, and small cutouts may need to be altered or eliminated because of potential breakage.

Very close lines can be separated slightly without making a difference in the overall design. (See Illustration 4.)

Long extended lines can be widened or shortened to give them strength. (See Illustration 5.)

Several small cuts can be connected to make one large cut. Some areas can be eliminated entirely. (See Illustration 6.)

Veining, the dead-end cut left by the width of the tablesaw, will give definition. Remember, if veining is

connected at both ends, it becomes a cut-out. (See Illustration 7.)

Because of the angle in relief cuts, care must be taken so that the pattern is not too close to the wood edge. Also, because relief work requires cutting in a certain direction, it is best to mark the pattern accordingly. Put a small "x" to mark the pilot hole and an arrow to show cutting direction. (See Illustration 8.)

The pilot hole should be as inconspicuous as possible. Therefore, hide it in the natural design of the cut. (See Illustration 9.)

The placement of pilot holes should not be too close to another part of the design. The angle of the pilot hole and the angle of the design can overlap, making it difficult to insert the blade. (See Illustration 10.)

GETTING STARTED

A right setting of three degrees is suggested on the following relief patterns. Suggested blade size is 12.5 teeth per inch. Beginning scrollers may want to start with the patterns on pages 8, 9, 15 and 29.

Illustration 9: Make the pilot hole as inconspicuous as possible. It can be hidden in the natural design of the cut.

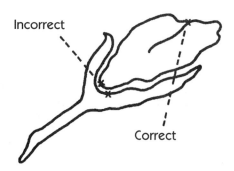

Illustration 10: Do not place the pilot hole for one part of the design close to another part of the design. Notice the placement of the correct and incorrect cuts above.

RELIEF

Practicing cuts before you begin on a pattern is always a good idea. Follow the directions on these two pages to familiarize yourself with relief cutting.

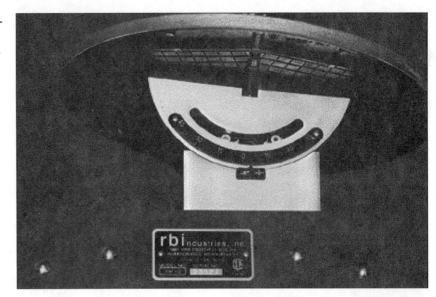

Choose a degree setting of 1°, 3° or 5°. Use either a right or left table set.

Using the practice sheet on the next page, make a practice cut following the directional arrows. Reset the saw and make the other cuts.

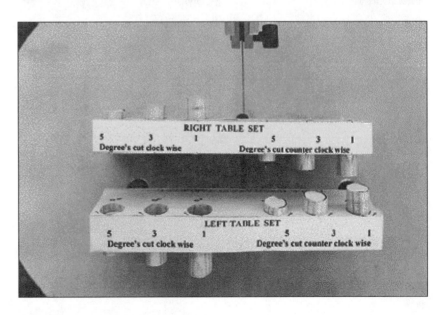

This picture shows the results of both a right and a left table set.

RELIEF

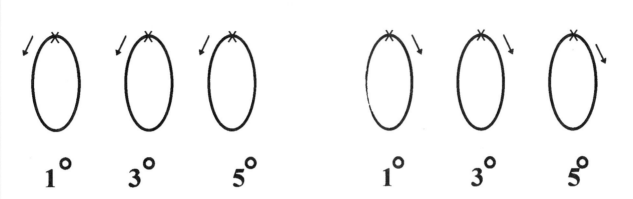

1°   3°   5°   1°   3°   5°

Practice sheet using a right table set.

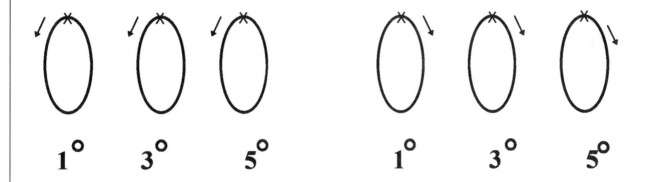

1°   3°   5°   1°   3°   5°

Practice sheet using a left table set.

This exercise will help you understand the relationship of four things—blade size, degrees, direction of the table set (right or left), and the direction of the cutting (clockwise or counterclockwise)—to the success of a relief cut. Start with 3/4-inch wood and a 12.5 tpi blade size, then change the width of the wood and the blade size to see the different effects.

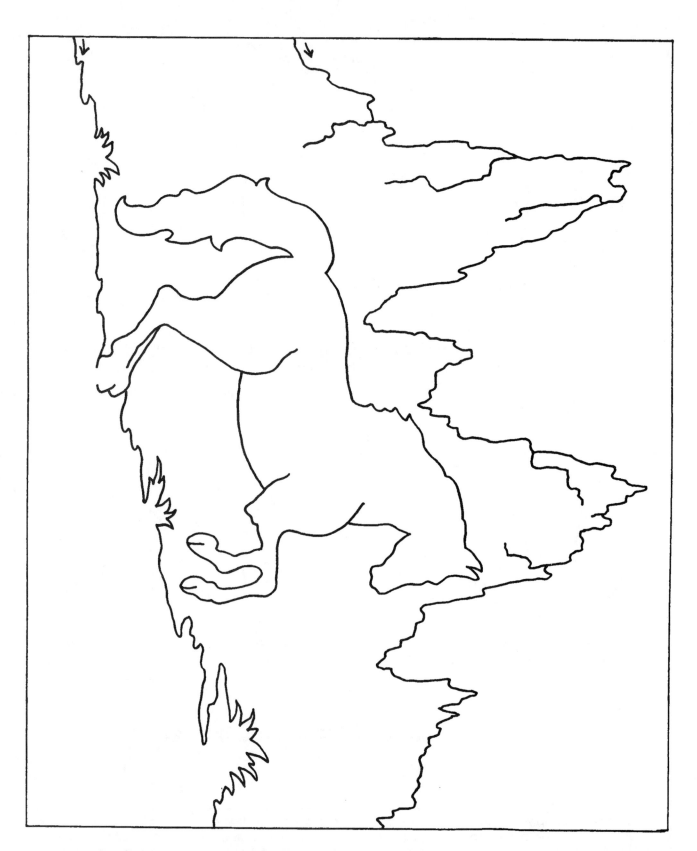

The relief cuts for these first two patterns are cut from the edge of the wood. These projects are excellent beginner relief projects.

SCROLL SAW RELIEF

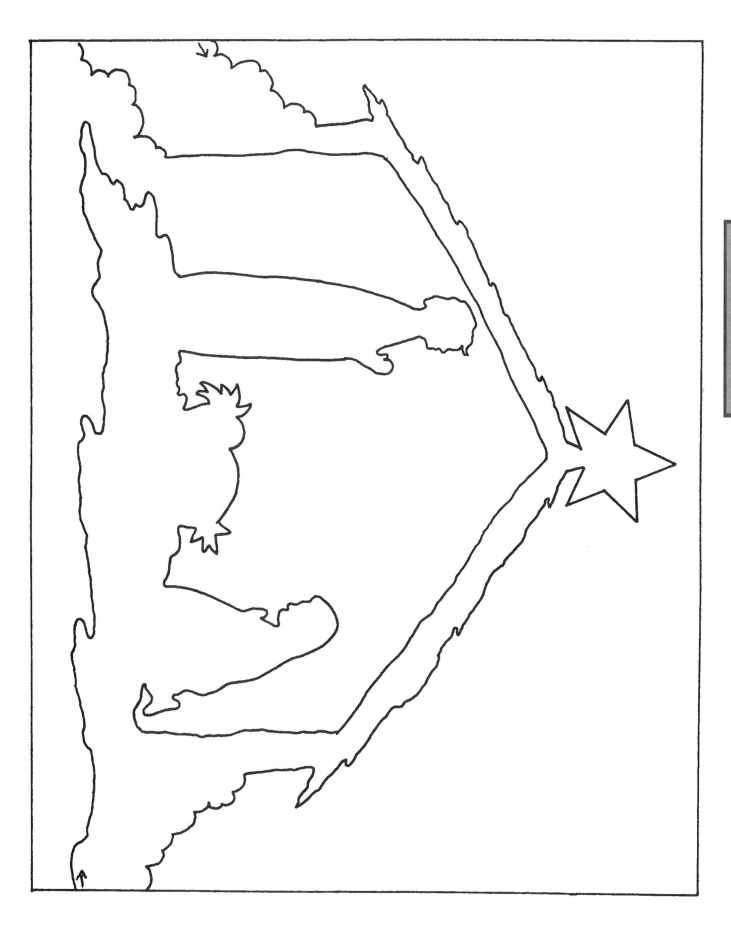

SCROLL SAW RELIEF

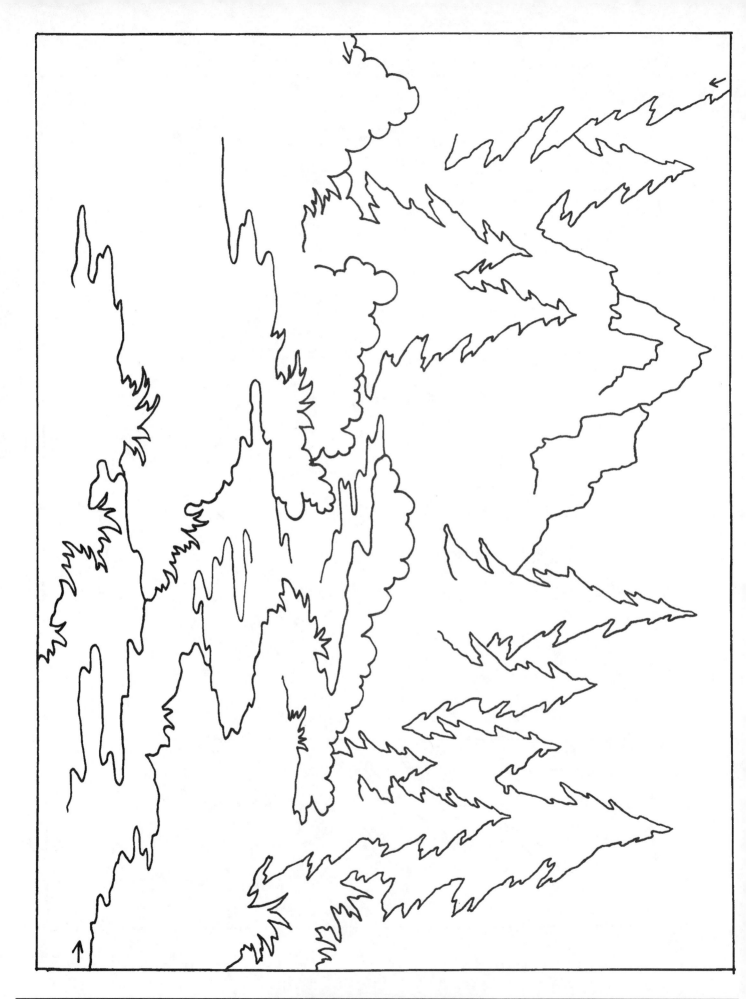

SCROLL SAW RELIEF

A teddy bear makes a fun addition to a child's room.

SCROLL SAW RELIEF

This design would work well incorporated into a holiday project.

These three miniatures make nice jewelry. You will need to use wood $1/4$" or thinner and a 2/0 blade. Adjust the tilt of the table and test. You may need a 5–10° angle on the saw table.

SCROLL SAW RELIEF

SCROLL SAW RELIEF

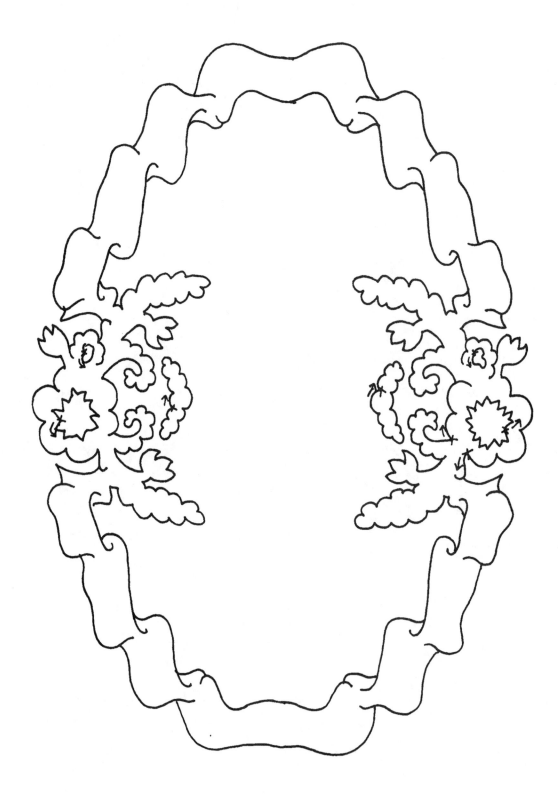

The top of a box is an excellent use for this ribbon and floral pattern.

SCROLL SAW RELIEF

This design, when placed in an oval with the center of the heart cut out, makes a lovely wedding or valentine frame.

SCROLL SAW RELIEF

SCROLL SAW RELIEF

RELIEF

A

B

Although not a beginner's pattern, this basket of flowers adds a touch of spring to any home.

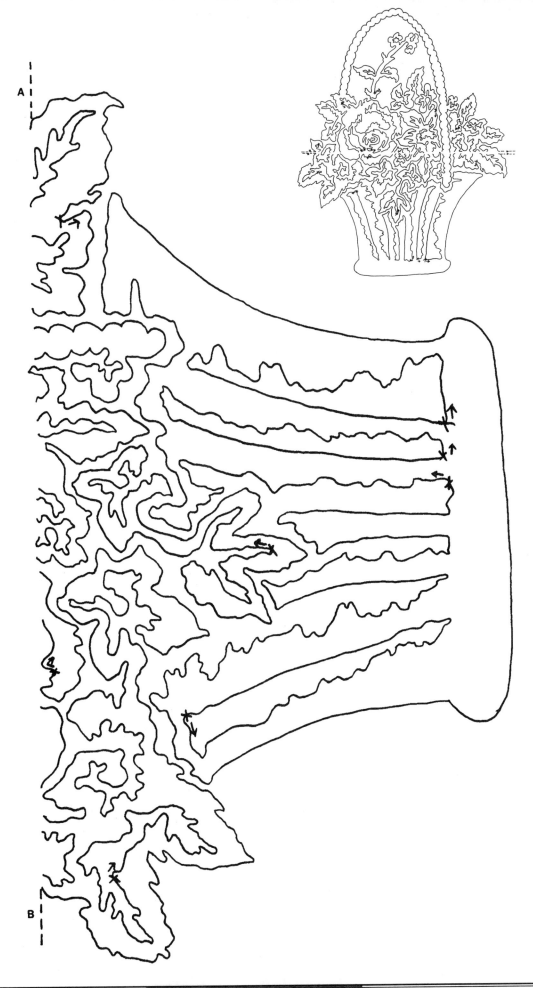

A

B

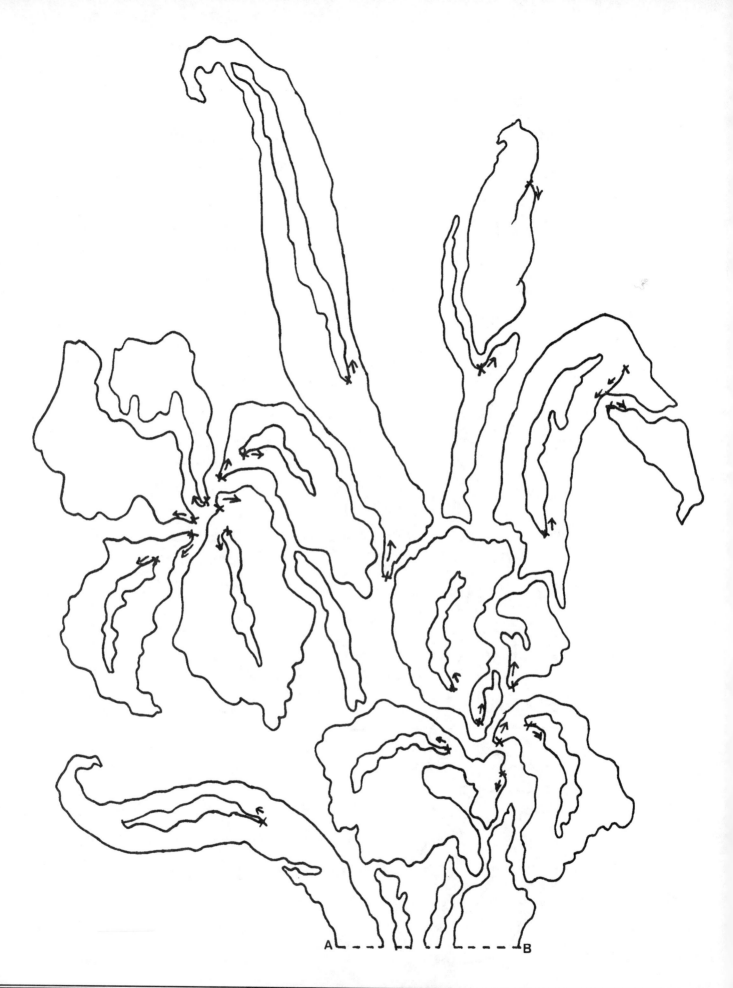

A - - - - - - - - - - - - B

SCROLL SAW RELIEF

Try these Iris on a finished cupboard door.

SCROLL SAW RELIEF

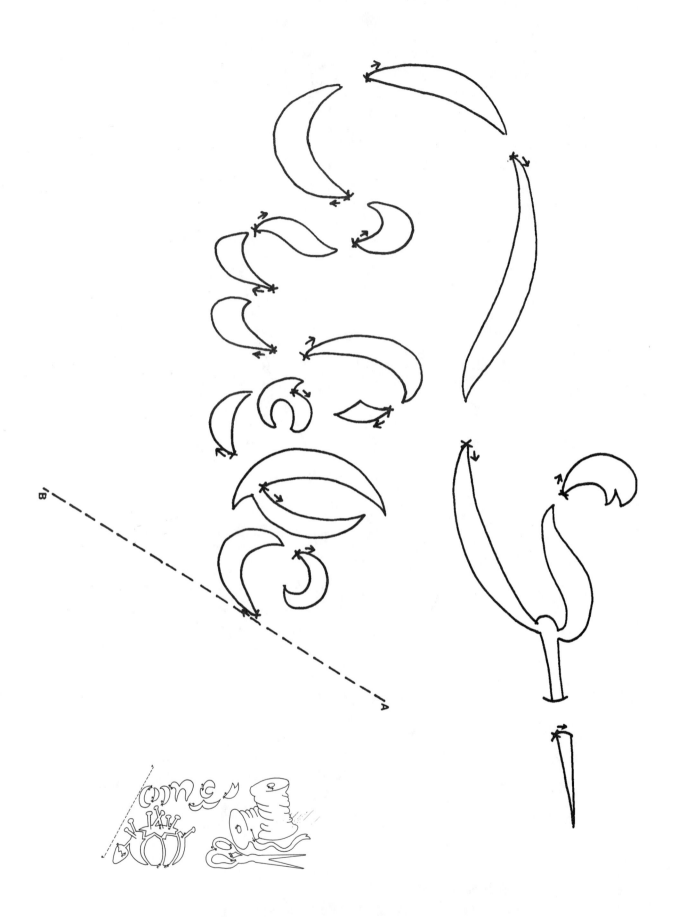

SCROLL SAW RELIEF

Finished in a dark wood, this picture frame has a Victorian look.

SCROLL SAW RELIEF

This design is a good accent for square or rectangular projects. Reverse the design for a right and left pattern.

SCROLL SAW RELIEF

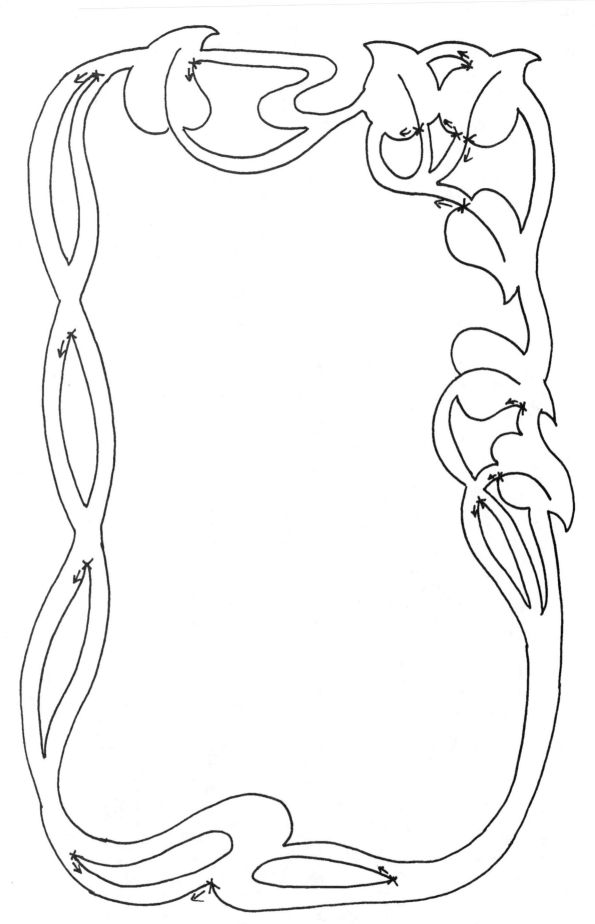

This stylized ivy is a great complement to the lid of a rectangle box.

SCROLL SAW RELIEF

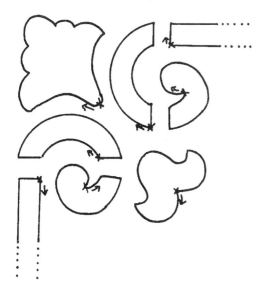

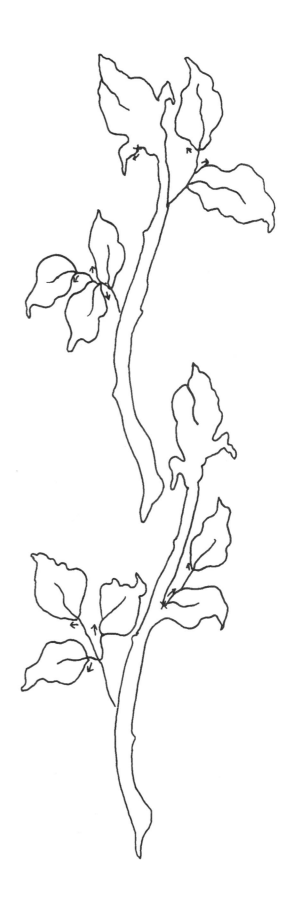

The following designs can be adjusted in size for borders around any project.

SCROLL SAW RELIEF

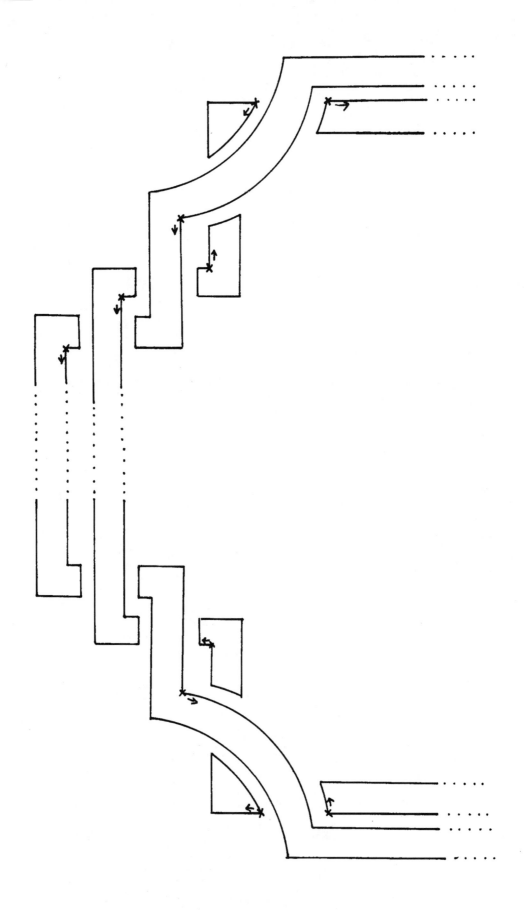

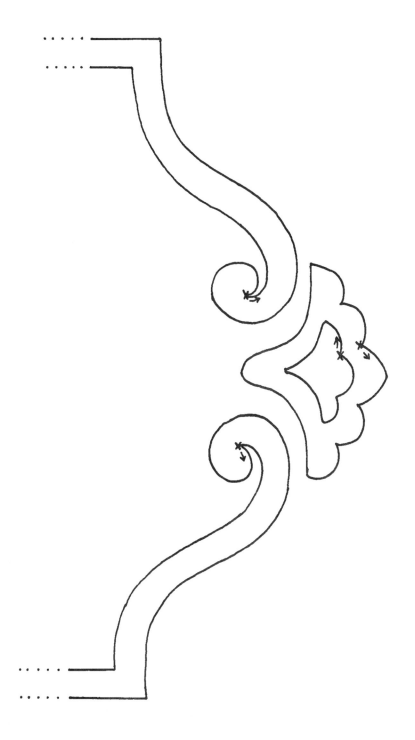

An excellent design for a picture frame.

SCROLL SAW RELIEF

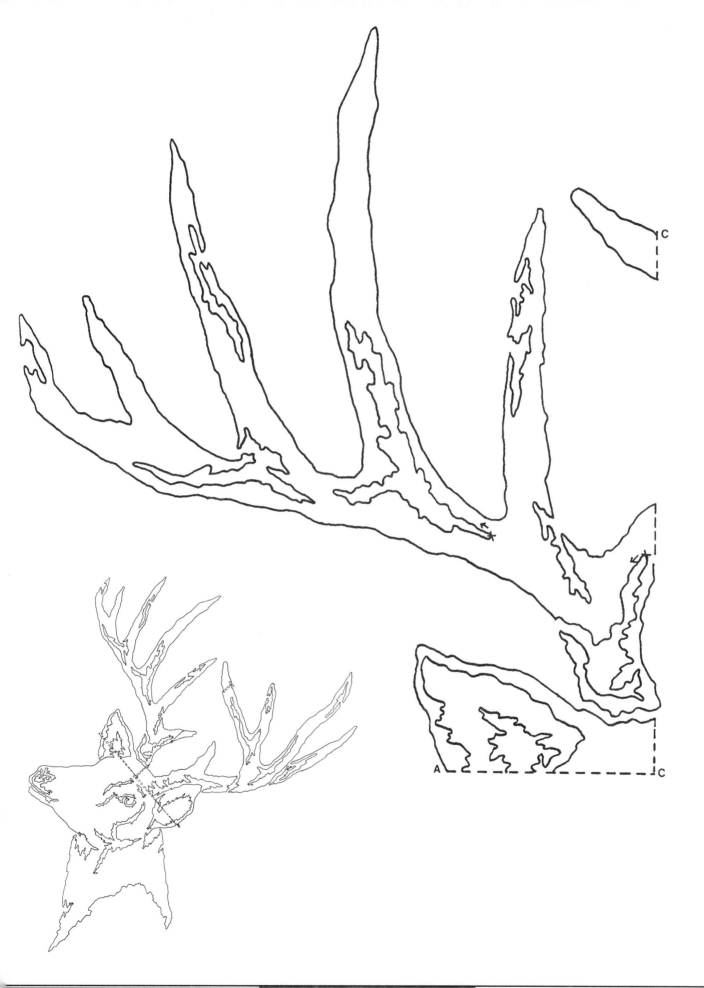

C

A ------------------------ C

SCROLL SAW RELIEF

A

B

SCROLL SAW RELIEF

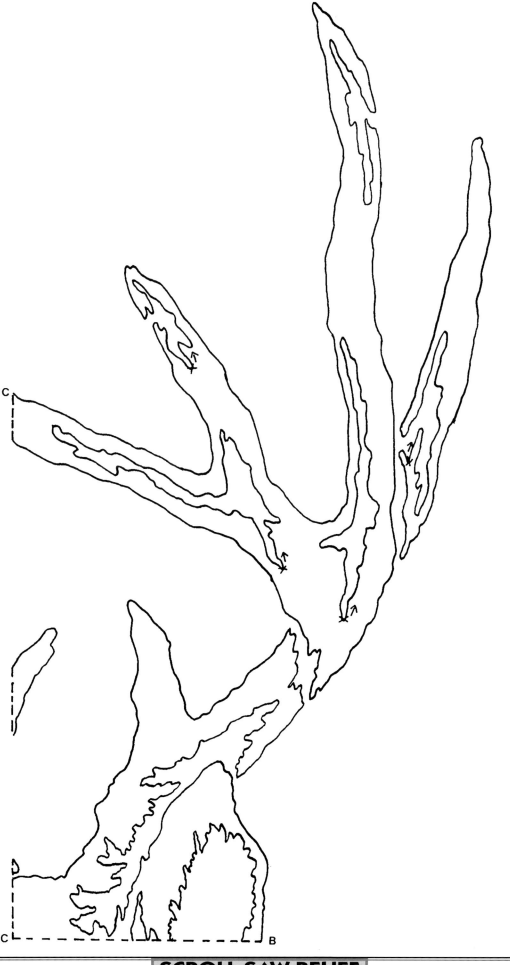

SCROLL SAW RELIEF

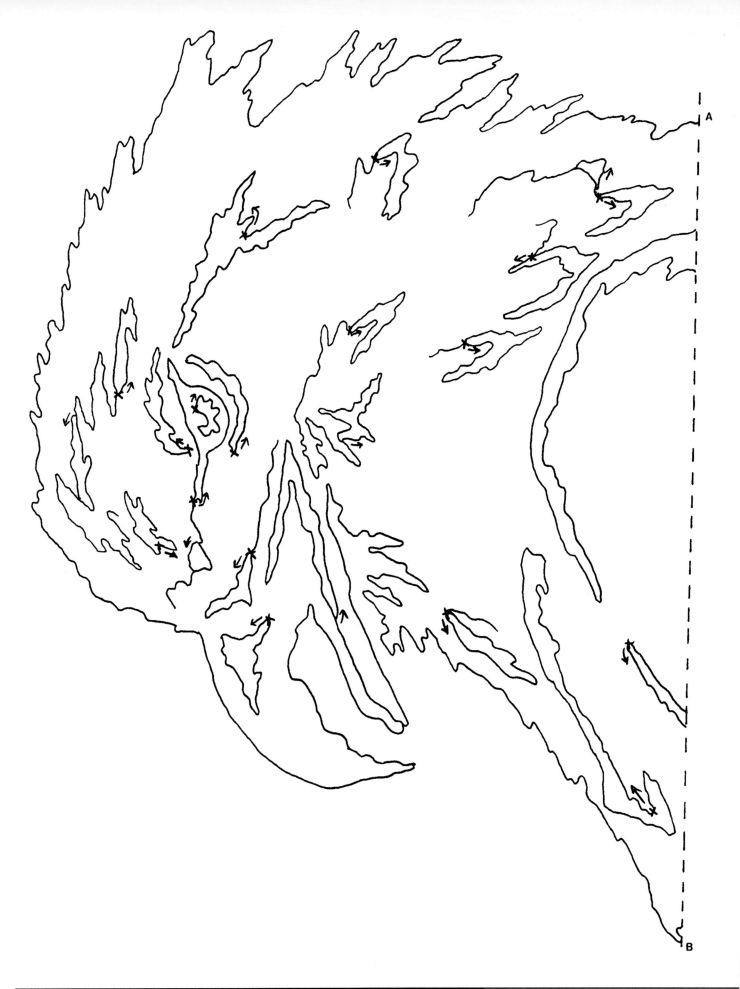

A

B

SCROLL SAW RELIEF

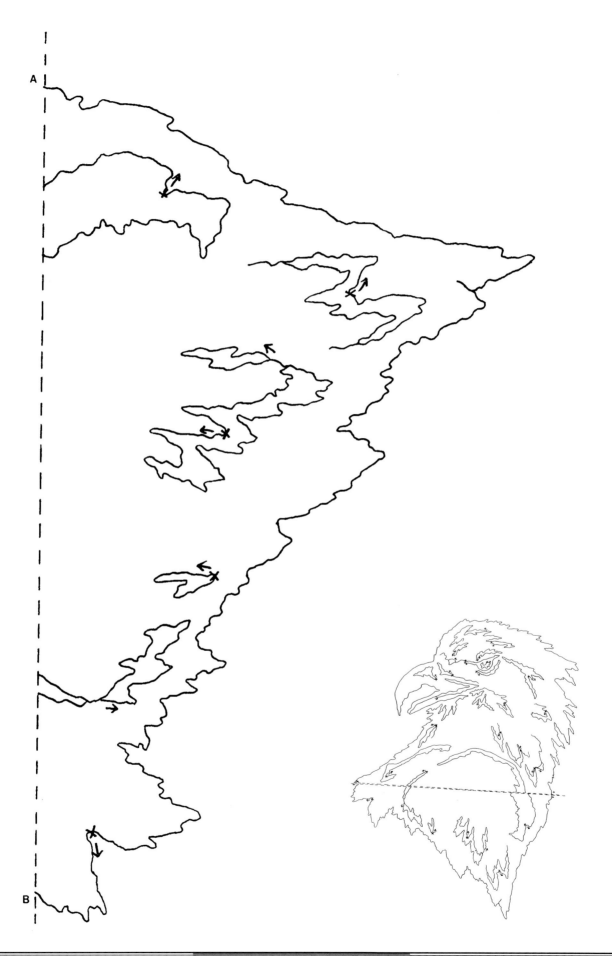

A

B

Fret Cutting

Fret designs often have a delicate, lacy look to them. In fret work, shadow, movement, definition and depth are all achieved by the shape and placement of cut-out areas. Fret work can enhance furniture, picture frames, shelves and clocks, and is often seen on the eaves of older homes. A good understanding of fret is needed when combining fret with relief techniques.

Contrasting wood adds a finished look to "Mary's Lamb" pull toy.

A lone loon resting in the shadow of cattails is cut from a redwood burl.

Pride and freedom of spirit are evident in this wild horse.

PART 2 • Technique

CHAPTER PURPOSE

To give a review of the proper techniques of fret cutting and to provide the basis for combining fret work with relief cutting.

TECHNIQUE

As with relief cutting, the scroll saw you use can put limitations on cutting fret designs. Saws requiring pin-end blades prevent cutting patterns with intricate designs. The pilot hole needs to be larger than the pins, eliminating small cuts.

Another limitation is found in the hold-down foot on some saws. It has some "give" or "spring" to it. This allows the foot to catch on previous cuts, causing breakage.

A third limitation is the throat depth of the saw. Any fret work longer than two times the saw throat will need to be done in sections and pieced together.

One of the biggest limitations for fret work is a saw that is frustrating to use. When it is difficult to release and reset the blade for inside cuts, those cuts will be avoided. Now all the fun of fret work has been missed!

After the pattern is placed on the wood, pilot holes need to be drilled. If a drill press is available, use it. This ensures straight drilling. If a hand drill is used, keep it as straight as possible. Pilot holes are drilled in the center of each cut-out. When possible, place the hole near a corner or angle. This gives a good starting point for cutting. (See Illustration 11.)

It is always easiest to insert the blade through large pilot holes. Use a large drill bit when possible, but a smaller one when necessary.

Fret is cut with the table flat, or square to the blade, (0 degrees). The blade size is dependent on the wood width and the intricacy of the design.When cutting fret, start with the smallest cuts and work up to the largest. This will help prevent breakage from your hands moving across the work. When the cuts are around the same size, start at the center and work out, or at one edge and work across. When the design has very fragile areas, cut these last. Be aware of your hand placement and where you apply pressure; the wrong spot can break the project.

In fret, the outside of the design is the final cut finishing the project. When fret is combined with relief, the outside of the design is often a relief cut. This gives the project a raised or recessed position within the surrounding wood.

Many designs have areas that are more intricate and delicate than the rest. Using a smaller blade for these areas will ensure a nicer and more "finished" piece.

Fret work can be cut in various widths and types of wood. The width of the wood is determined by how the design is to be used and by whether relief is being incorporated into the fret design. For example, gingerbread decorations for eaves on a home would be cut from a thicker wood than a design used as a wall plaque.

Illustration 12: Positive and negative fret designs.

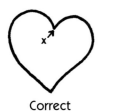

Correct   Incorrect

Illustration 11: It is best to start cutting at a corner or angle.

Illustration 13: Veining used to give definition between two cut-outs.

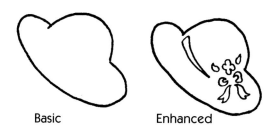

Basic   Enhanced

Illustration 14: Fret can enhance a basic shape.

HINTS FOR FRET PATTERNS

Creating a fret design can be not only challenging, but also loads of fun. The following will help when designing fret patterns or adding fret to a relief pattern.

Limit the detail of a design to cuts that create the pattern. There is no sense in doing in-depth cuts that add nothing to the overall design.

A design can be achieved with both "positive" and "negative" cuts. (See Illustration 12.)

Veining gives definition and is often used between two cut-out areas. (See Illustration 13).

Wide-open cutouts seldom look as good cut as they do on the pattern. This does not mean that you shouldn't use them. Just be aware. This is often an excellent area to change to a relief cut.

Definition, shading and depth can be added to a pattern with the placement of a fret or relief cut. A combination of the two is also very effective. (See Illustration 14.) You'll find more information on combining fret and relief in Part 3.

Often the design does not "cut" as planned. When doing your own designs, remember that some changes may be necessary. The first time a new design is cut, it can be used as a test pattern. Weak areas are often revealed after cutting. Simple design changes can add the needed strength. With experience will come understanding of pattern design, helping to eliminate some of these needed changes.

GETTING STARTED

Beginning scrollers will want to start with the patterns on pages 46, 47, 50, 54 and 74.

This piece of fret is patterned after Liberty, a bald eagle whose injuries prevent him from being released into the wild. He and his handler now educate people about these magnificent birds.

A light catcher draws attention to this heart. Here, the heart is cut from 3/8-inch black walnut.

A child's love of ponies is evident in this design.

As you can see by the X's and directional arrows, this pattern was originally planned as a relief pattern. But by ignoring these markings, you can easily change this pattern into a fret pattern. You'll find that the majority of the patterns in this book are interchangeable. This frame—carved in relief or fret—works well for a mirror or a picture.

Hanging a name from the horseshoe turns this design into a plaque for a child's room.

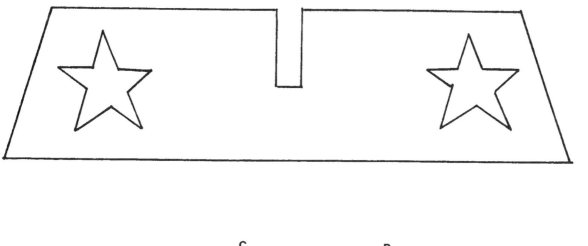

C - - - - - - - - - D

For a free-standing clown, slide one base into the second.

This small pull-toy is assembled using doweling to attach wheels and 1/8" ribbon from pull handle to neck.

A prism, hung in the center, adds sparkle and movement to this heart.

SCROLL SAW RELIEF

A touch of style is added when this design is used as a shelf bracket

This design is different in that it is cut in the negative. What is cut away makes the design show up.

SCROLL SAW RELIEF

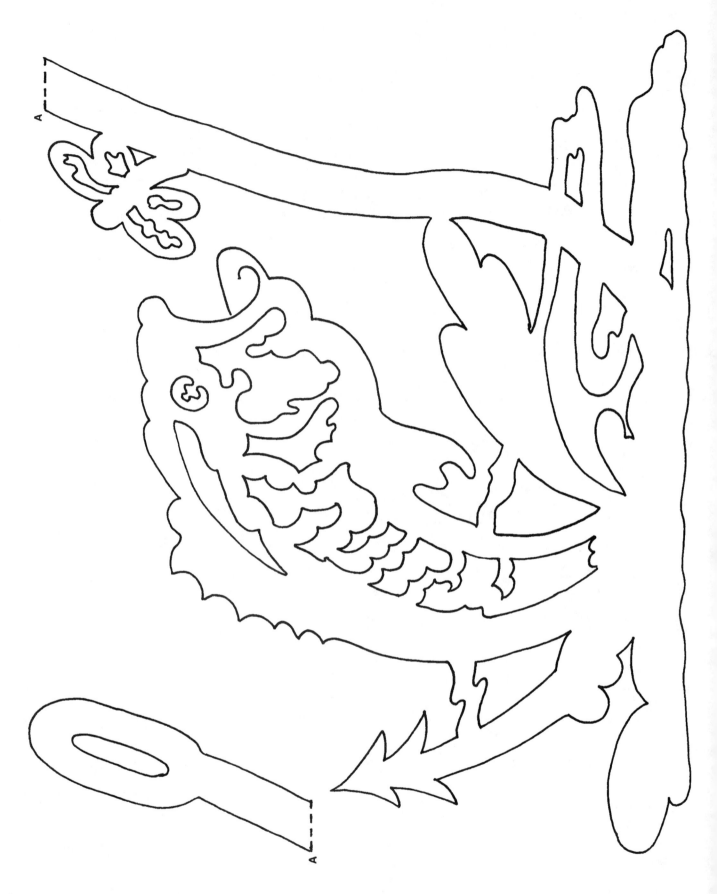

A fun design for the fisherman in the family.

SCROLL SAW RELIEF

FRET

Y

SCROLL SAW RELIEF

A

B

Z

U

SCROLL SAW RELIEF

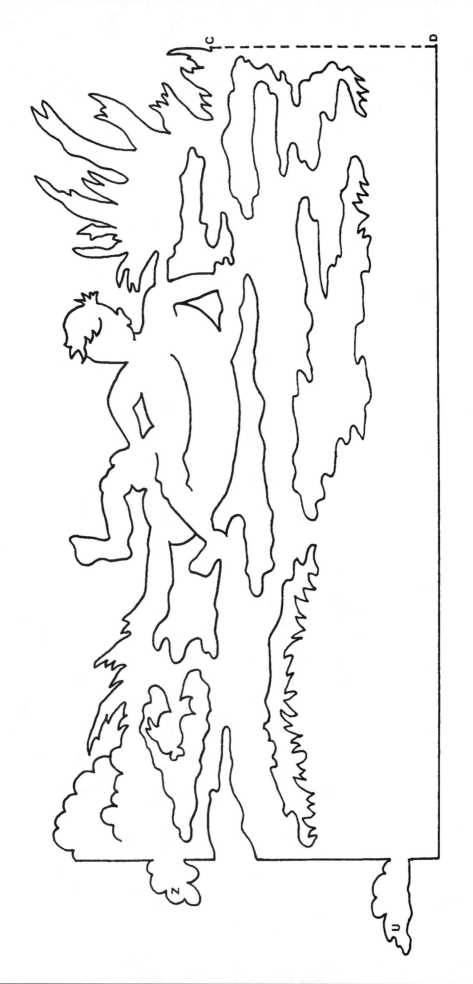

SCROLL SAW RELIEF

SCROLL SAW RELIEF

Frame the foreground and background as one for your Barbershop Quartet.

SCROLL SAW RELIEF

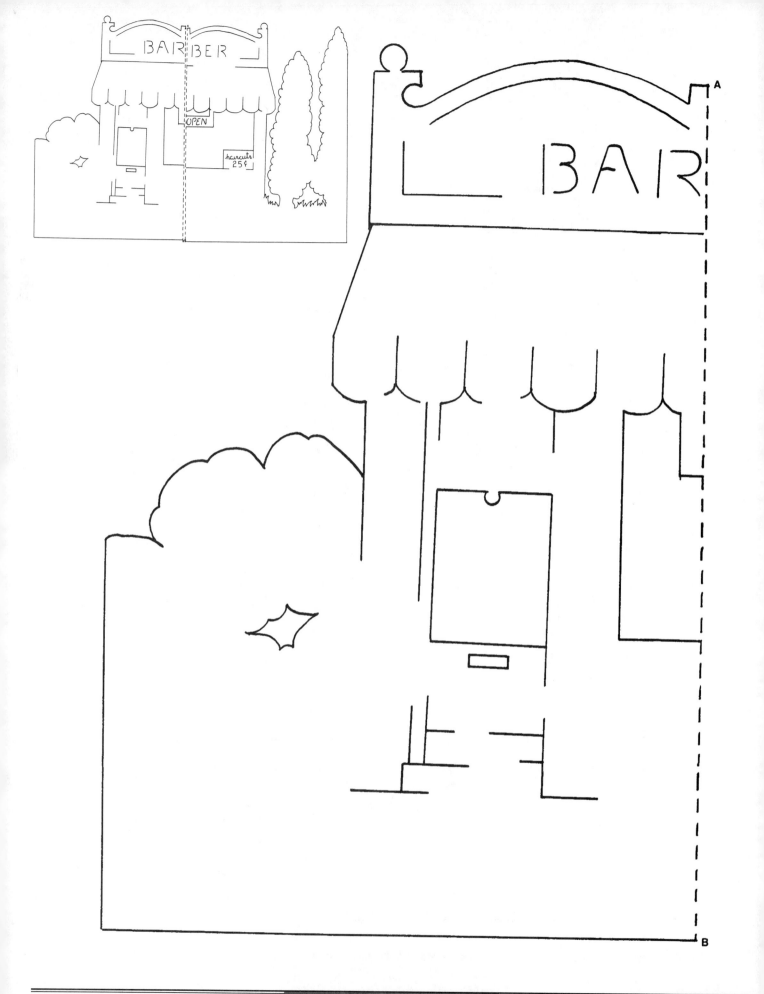

SCROLL SAW RELIEF

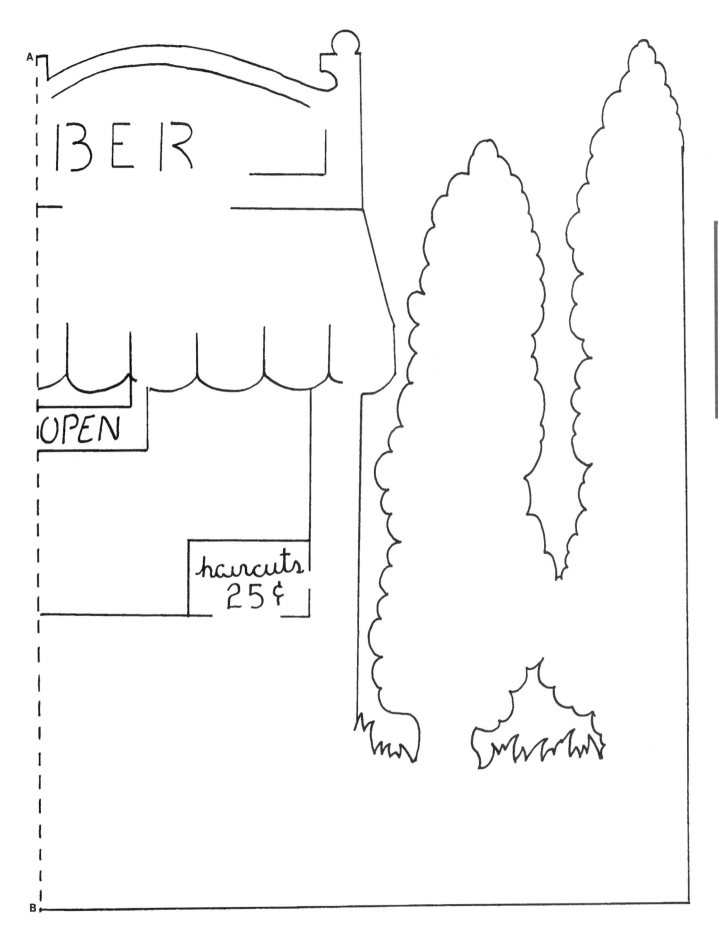

A

BER

OPEN

haircuts
25¢

B

SCROLL SAW RELIEF

SCROLL SAW RELIEF

This pattern is awesome enlarged 200–300%.

SCROLL SAW RELIEF

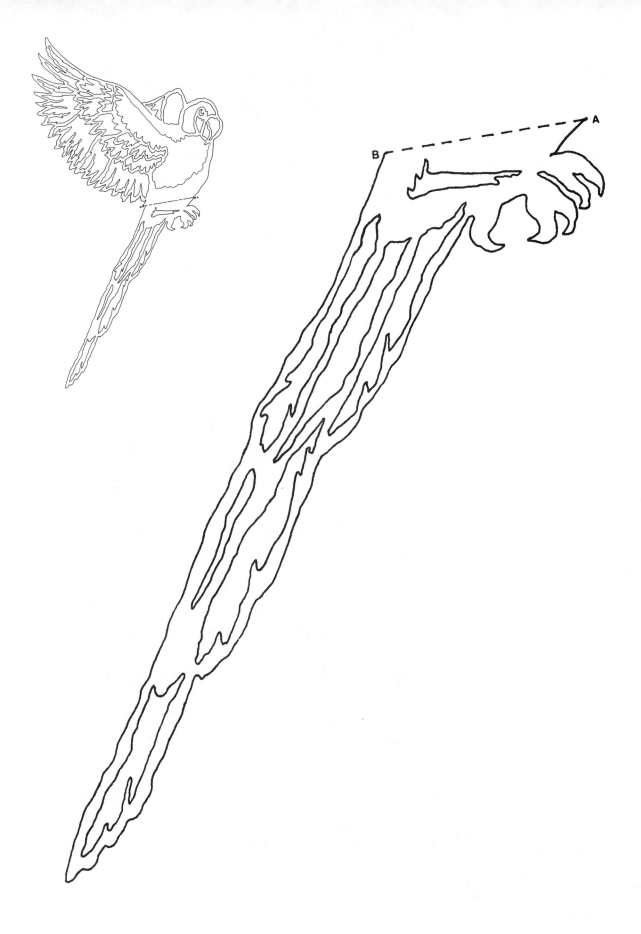

Try cutting this parrot from a piece of colorful plastic.

SCROLL SAW RELIEF

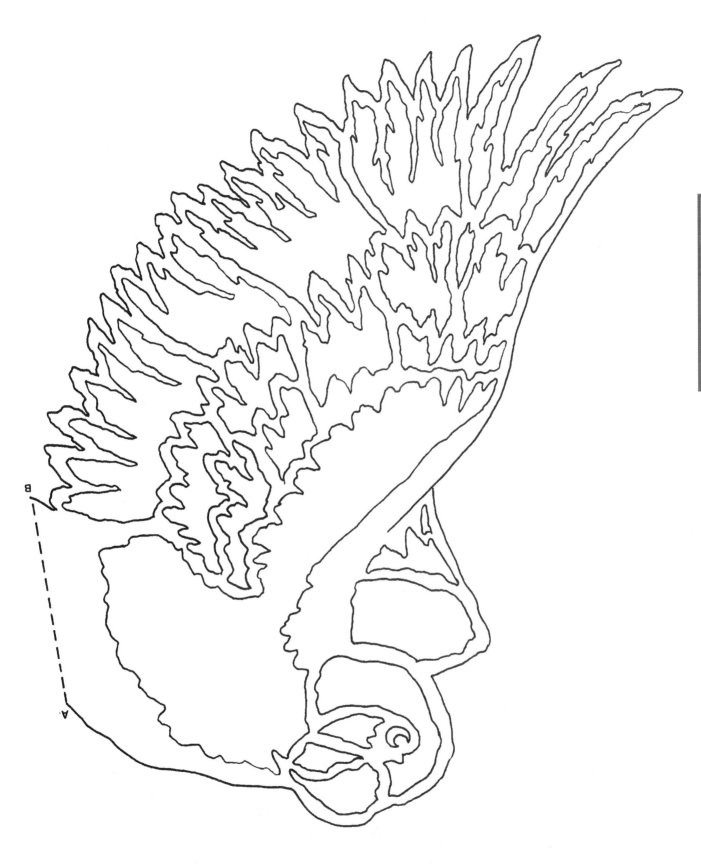

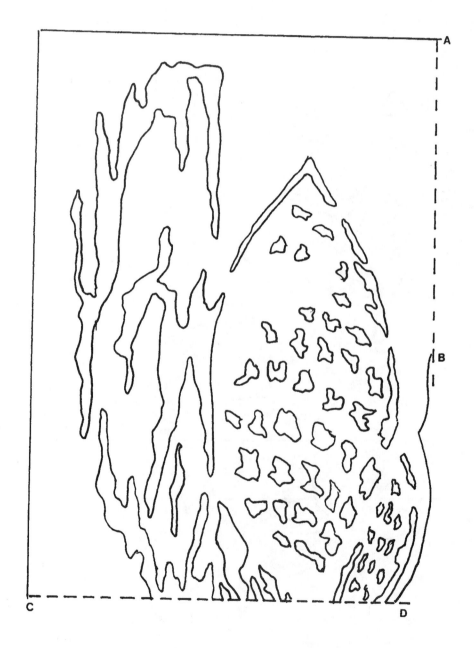

A

B

C   D

The following loon looks real nice on an irregular piece of wood.

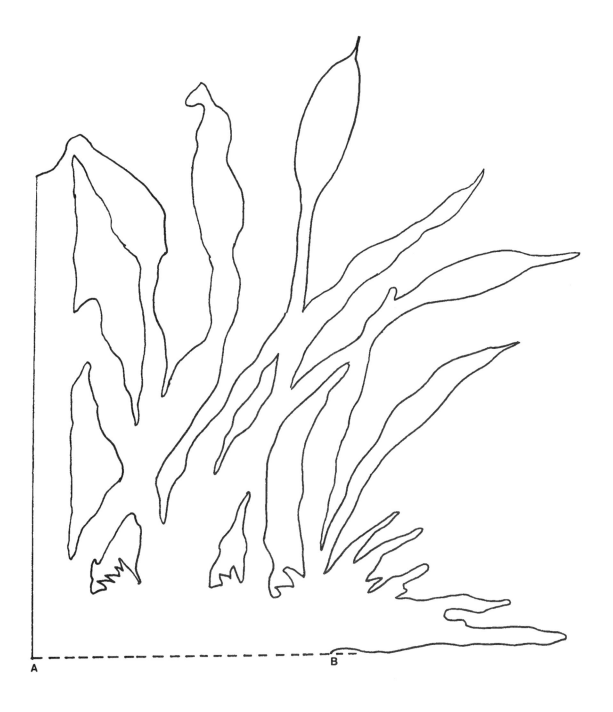

A

B

SCROLL SAW RELIEF

C   D

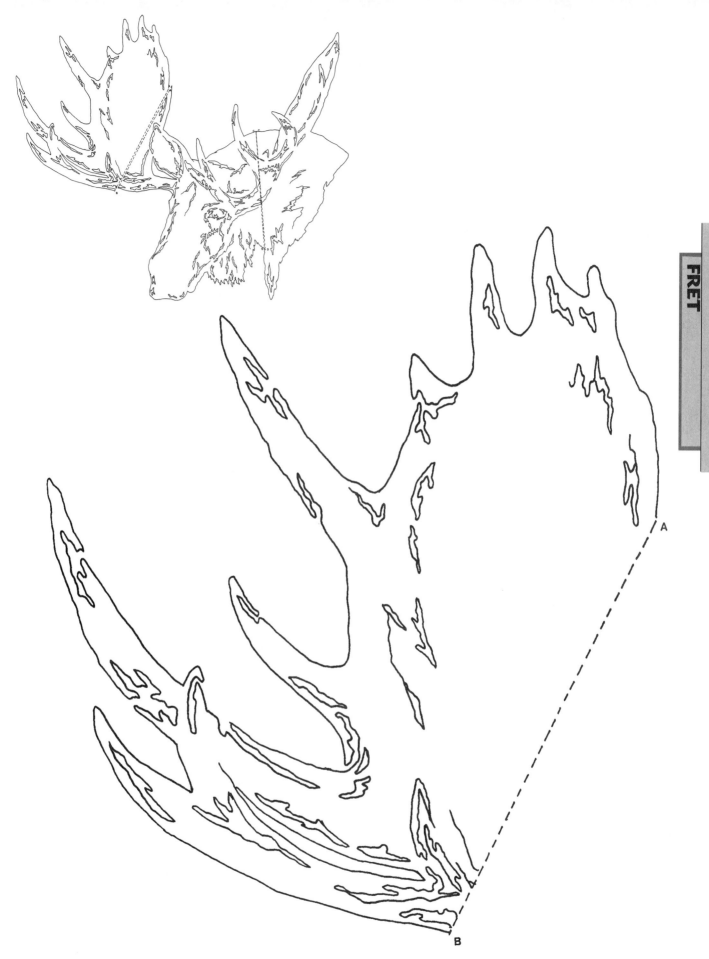

A piece of rough and weathered wood adds to the "natural" look of this moose.

SCROLL SAW RELIEF

SCROLL SAW RELIEF

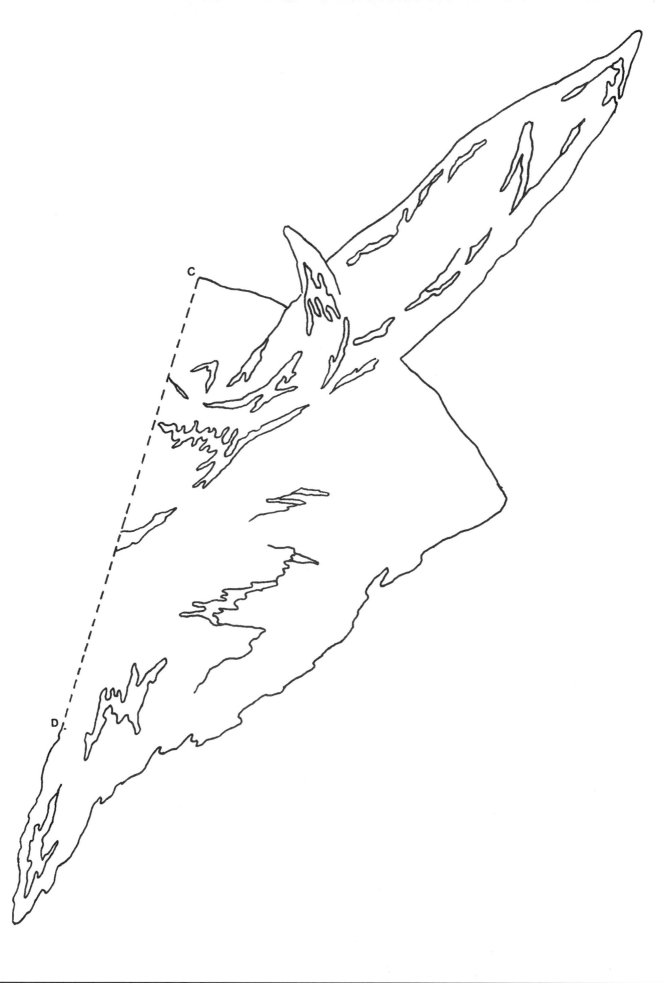

C

D

SCROLL SAW RELIEF

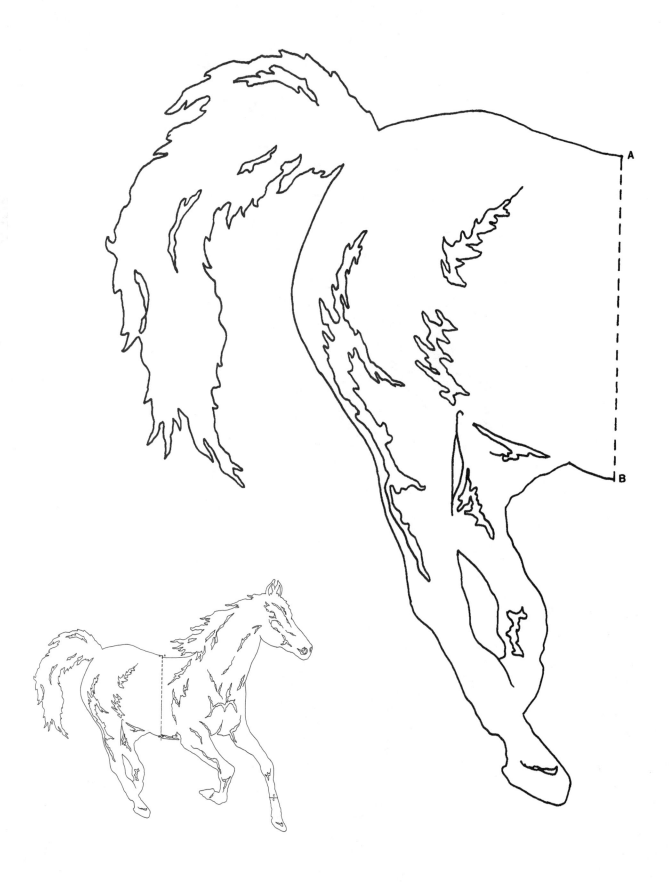

Different grained woods give this horse a totally new look.

A

B

C

C

SCROLL SAW RELIEF

C

D

SCROLL SAW RELIEF

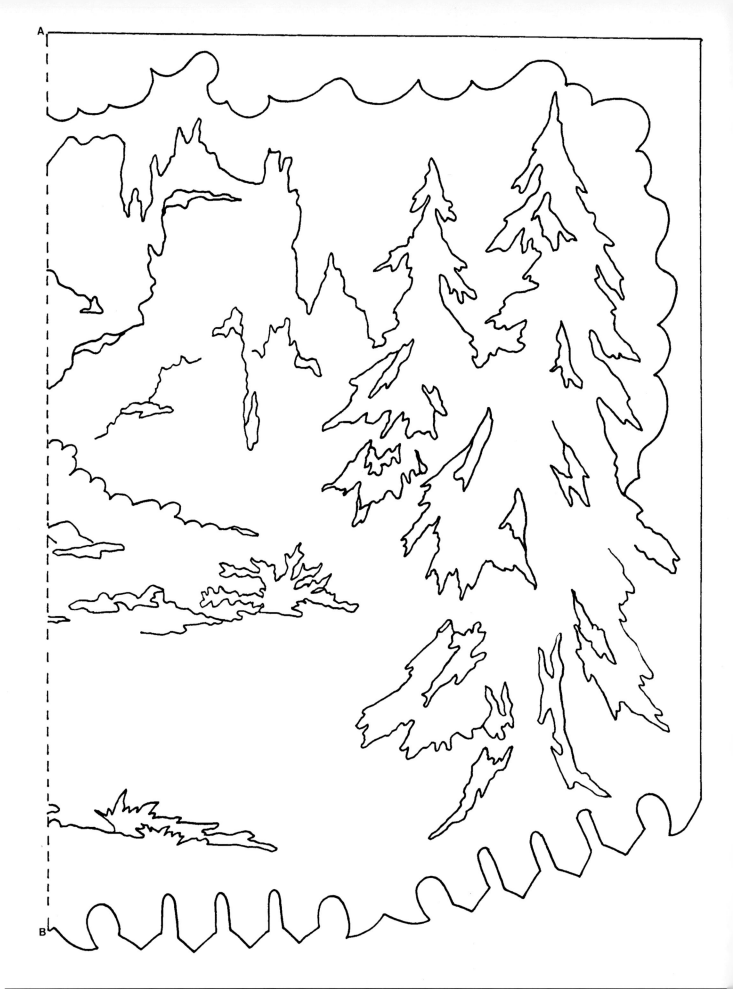

A

B

Combining Fret and Relief

Relief and fret cutting can be combined within the same project to create a truly unique look. The resulting finished piece incorporates the lacy look of fret cutting with the raised or recessed areas of relief cutting. These two techniques work well together on frames, ornaments and many other projects.

The *Apple Tree* combines both relief cutting and fret work. The apples have been recessed to draw attention to them.

This Christmas tree was cut from the sapwood of an English walnut. Several layers of relief combined with fret work give the tree added definition and character.

PART 3 • Technique

CHAPTER PURPOSE

To show how to combine relief and fret cutting to create combination patterns and projects employing both techniques.

TECHNIQUE

The technique for combination patterns is simply the use of relief and fret cutting within a single project.

As in relief designs and fret designs, combination projects are also limited to the throat depth of the saw being used. Because of the combination of techniques, several blade sizes may be needed. You'll need the appropriate blade for the relief, plus other blade sizes appropriate for the wood and intricacy of the fret areas.

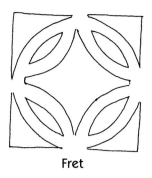 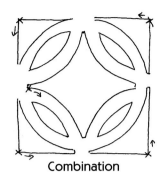

Fret   Combination

Illustration 17: Small changes give a different look to a fret pattern.

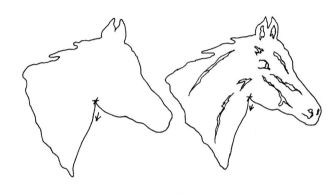

Illustration 16: Fret can add bone structure to a wildlife relief.

Basic relief   Basic relief with fret added

Illustration 15: Fret added to enhance a relief project.

Cutting should always start with the smaller fret areas, working to the larger. All fret areas within a relief area need to be cut first. Cut the relief after finishing the fret. The exception to this is when the fret area is exceptionally large or vulnerable to breakage. In this case, cut it last.

Small and intricate fret areas may need to be enlarged or simplified to convert them to a relief cut.

Caution: Do not put the relief cut too close to the fret cut. If you do, the angle on the relief will cut through the edge of the fret areas.

HINTS

Changing a relief or a fret pattern into a combination can greatly enhance the original. The simplest change is made by using a basic shape and adding it to a plaque or sign. The only step needed is to turn the shape's outside edge into a relief cut.

With fret added to a relief pattern or relief cuts changed to fret, an otherwise plain pattern is turned into a more delicate and pleasing design. (See Illustration 15.) A particularly good place to add fret is wildlife or animal patterns. Fret added to a basic relief silhouette can define muscle and bone structure. (See Illustration 16.)

Fret patterns can also be made into a combination. Sometimes, small changes are all it takes. (See Illustration 17.) Large background areas of fret design are often excellent areas to turn into a "recessed" relief cut.

GETTING STARTED

Beginning scrollers may want to start with the patterns on pages 93, 96, 100, 107 and 108. Lines that are marked with a directional arrow and an X are relief cuts. All other cuts are fret.

This combination pattern resembles a quilt. Try using a colored background behind the finished piece.

COMBINATION

Hannah Grace, an angel of beauty, uses a combination of fret, relief and veining techniques.

Maggie, a cougar living in a wildlife rehabilitation center in Oregon, inspired this project. Although pictured here as a fret project, the pattern also makes an excellent combination project. The pattern is found in this chapter.

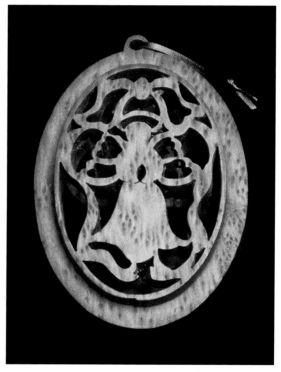

This Christmas ornament is cut from redwood. The relief cuts give the ornament a finished width of $2^{1}/_{2}"$.

COMBINATION

Many combination patterns can be used to accent signs.

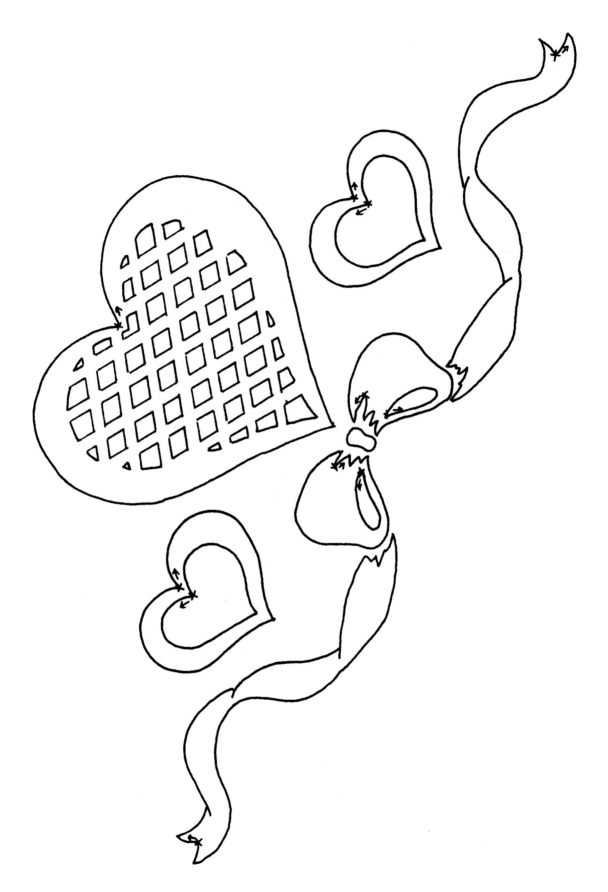

This is an excellent design to finish the back of a shelf.

SCROLL SAW RELIEF

For each ornament, cut two of pattern from 1/2" wood. Glue in relief. Finish the ornaments by gluing the two halves together.

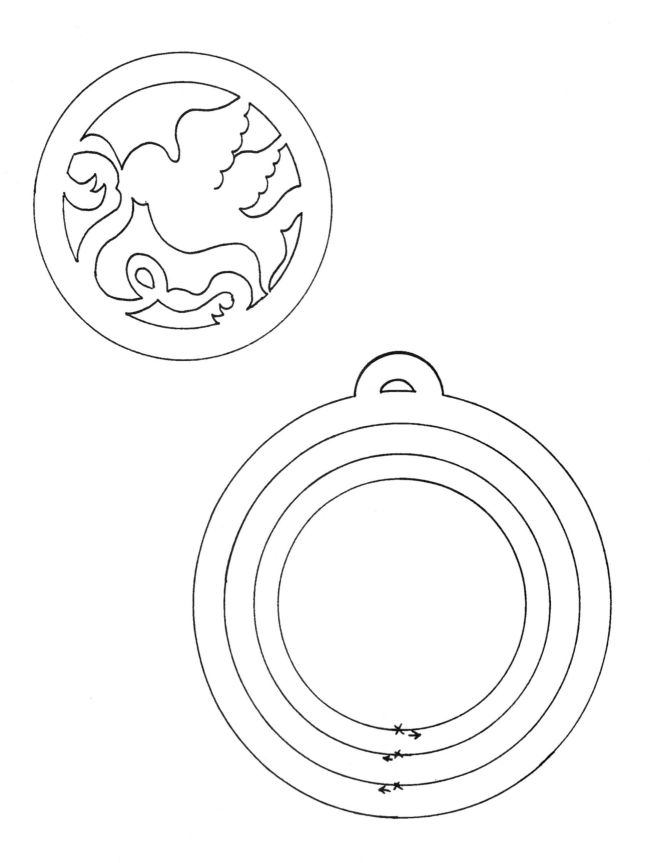

Cut two doves from ¹/₄" wood and two of the circle pattern from ¹/₂" wood. (Contrasting woods suggested.) Remove the center from each circle. Glue in relief with the doves in the centers. Finish the ornament by gluing the two circles back-to-back.

SCROLL SAW RELIEF

For something different, use the apples to frame photographs for a family tree.

A

B

SCROLL SAW RELIEF

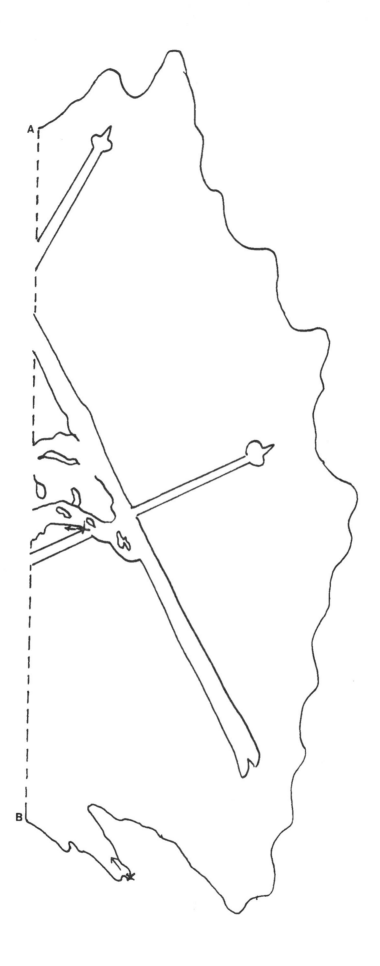

This and the following design can be used singly or together.

SCROLL SAW RELIEF

Chapter

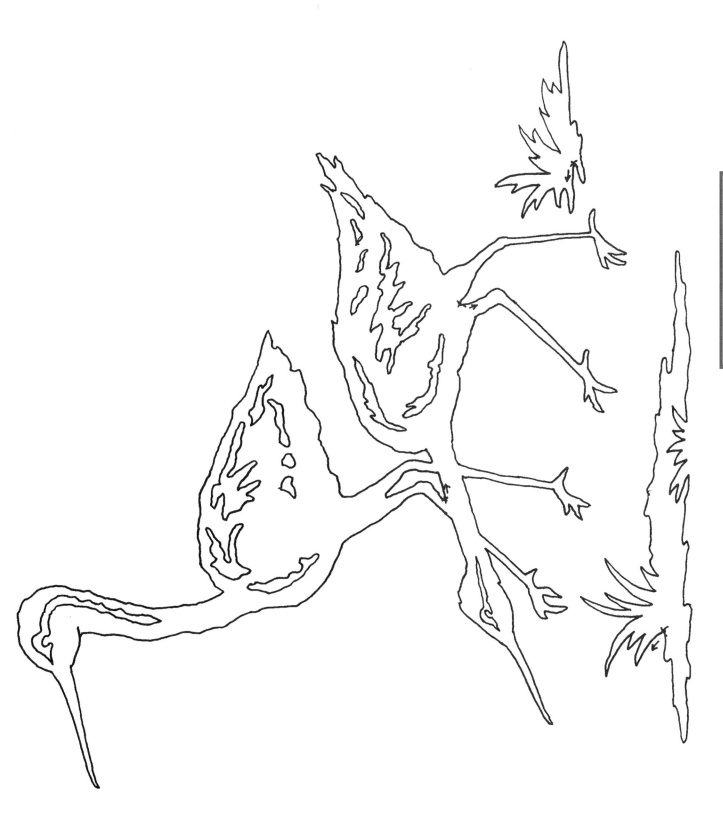

SCROLL SAW RELIEF

GRANDMA'S LOVE SERVED HERE

SCROLL SAW RELIEF

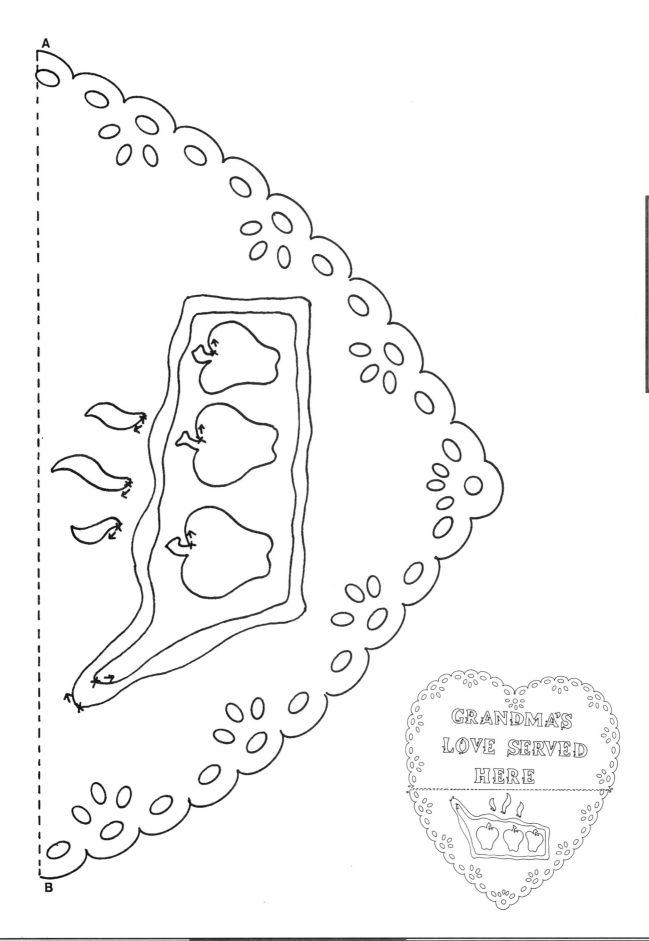

GRANDMA'S
LOVE SERVED
HERE

SCROLL SAW RELIEF

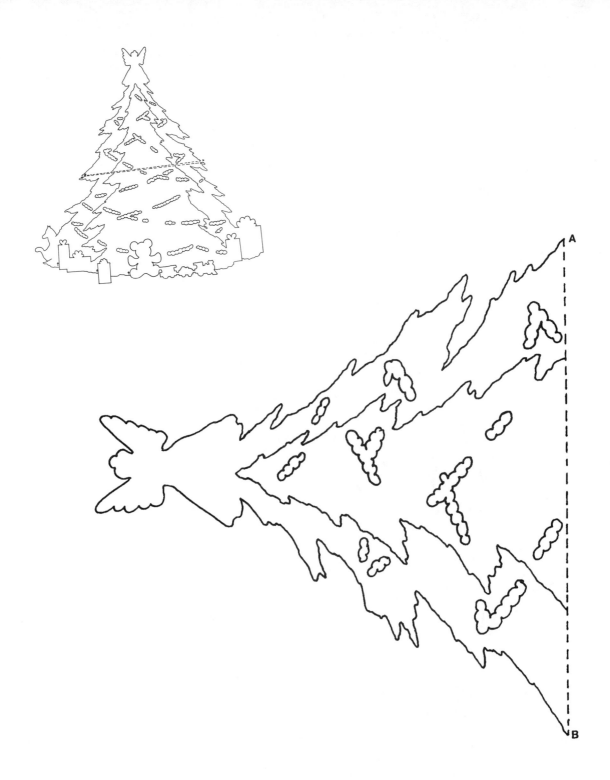

For something different, make this tree free-standing by cutting two trees, (a right and a left) and gluing them back-to-back.

SCROLL SAW RELIEF

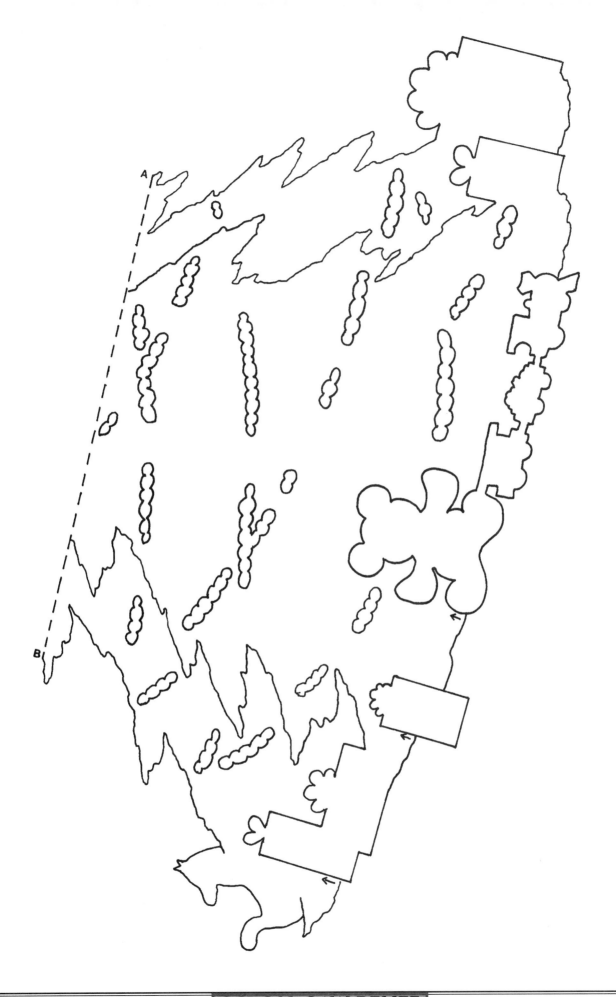

SCROLL SAW RELIEF

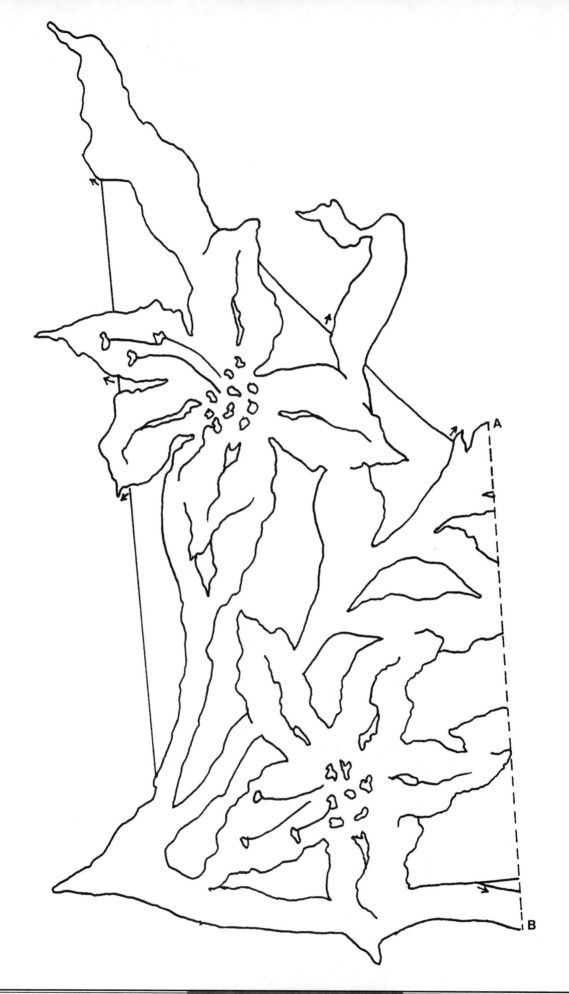

A

B

SCROLL SAW RELIEF

There is one relief cut on this pattern. When cutting, follow the arrow from "C" to "D." A suggested wood for this pattern is a hardwood burl.

A

C →

B

SCROLL SAW RELIEF

A

B

SCROLL SAW RELIEF

A

B

A

B

Frame is sized for a 5" x 7" mirror or picture.

SCROLL SAW RELIEF

A

C

COMBINATION

B

D

SCROLL SAW RELIEF

SCROLL SAW RELIEF

SCROLL SAW RELIEF

SCROLL SAW RELIEF

SCROLL SAW RELIEF

Afterword

My hope is that through these patterns I have been able to share my enthusiasm and love of scrolling. Relief work and fret combined with relief are probably my favorite scroll saw techniques! If you continue to discover the fun in scrolling, if you make one minor change to a pattern or if you begin designing full time, then the time and effort of this book have been worth it!

Sincerely,
Marilyn